FREAKS OF NATURE

Other books by John Callahan

Don't Worry, He Won't Get Far on Foot:
The Autobiography of a Dangerous Man

Do Not Disturb Any Further

Digesting the Child Within
and Other Cartoons to Live By

Do What He Says! He's Crazy!!!

I Think I Was an Alcoholic

The Night, They Say, Was Made for Love
plus My Sexual Scrapbook

What Kind of a God Would Allow
a Thing Like This to Happen?!!

The King of Things
and the Cranberry Clown

FREAKS OF NATURE

THE
"HONEST LAWYER"

Stay!

THE
"OBEDIENT CAT"

THE
"HAPPY-GO-LUCKY
FEMINIST"

JOHN CALLAHAN

QUILL
WILLIAM MORROW
NEW YORK

To Bob Newhart

Library of Congress Cataloging-in-Publication Data

Callahan, John.
    Freaks of nature / by John Callahan.
        p.   cm.
    ISBN 0-688-13338-X
    1. American wit and humor, Pictorial.   I. Title.
    NC1429.C23A4   1995
    741.5′973—dc20   95-34119
                                                                                    CIP

Printed in the United States of America

First Quill Edition

1 2 3 4 5 6 7 8 9 10

BOOK DESIGN BY ARLENE SCHLEIFER GOLDBERG

CALLAHAN

CALLAHAN

9

CONNIE CHUNG IN HER NEW CO-ANCHOR POSITION.

"What I have to tell you, Mrs. Carlson,
isn't easy to say. . . ."

"He's taking along a pair of old Levis to sell in Europe!"

CALLAHAN

CALLAHAN

19

IDIOTS ANONYMOUS

CALLAHAN

DON KING IS ELECTROCUTED...

CALLAHAN

"Are you still considering that nose job?!!"

"It's just that I've never engaged in foreplay
with a dairy farmer before."

CALLAHAN

Bobby Knight, age 2

CALLAHAN

"I think if I had it to do all over again,
I'd sit on this chair frontwards."

A DAY IN L.A.
YOUR CAR OR YOUR LIFE!
WELL... WHAT'S IT GONNA BE?!!
I'M THINKING!
CALLAHAN

CALLAHAN

CALLAHAN

CALLAHAN

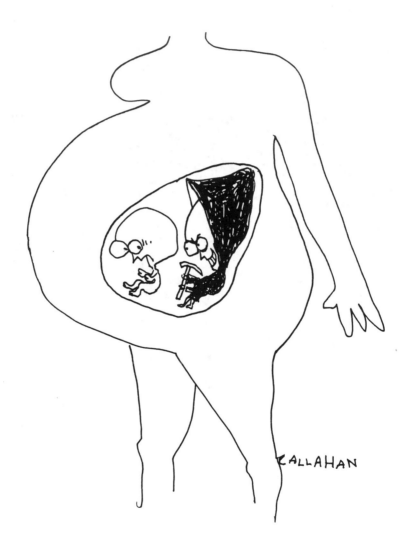

CALLAHAN

What is it that so depresses you about the expression: "you are what you eat"?
CALLAHAN

SCHIZOPHRENICS ANONYMOUS

CALLAHAN

"I take it the meal wasn't satisfactory."

NEWT DESCENDING A STAIRCASE

CALLAHAN

ANACONDOM

CALLAHAN

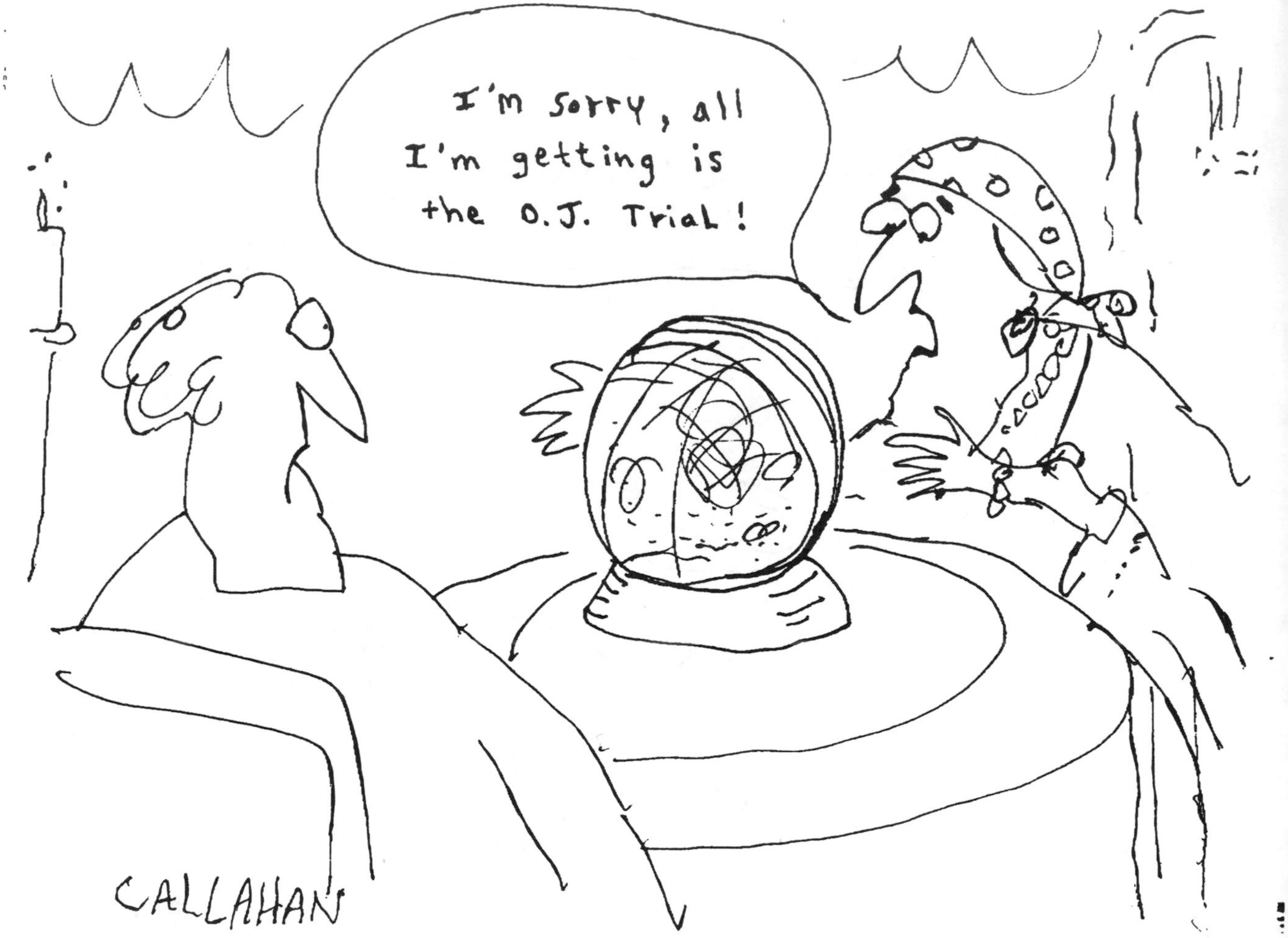
I'm sorry, all I'm getting is the O.J. Trial!
CALLAHAN

"I feel your pain."

Michael Jackson with his attorneys attempting to purchase all rights to the music of the spheres.

CALLAHAN

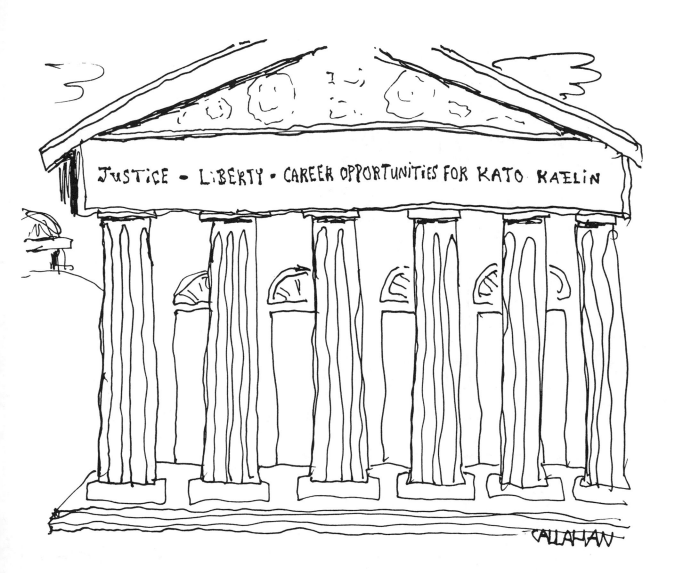

OBSESSIVE
COMPULSIVE
DISORDER
CLINIC

CALLAHAN

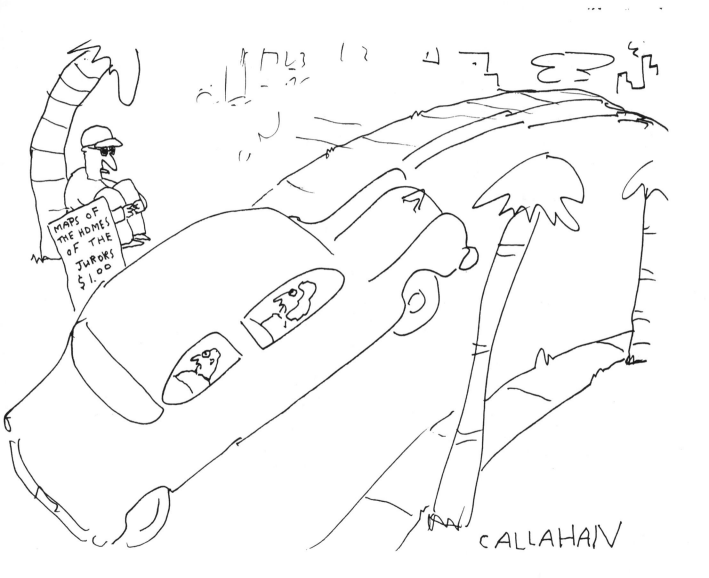

MAPS OF
THE HOMES
OF THE
JURORS
$1.00

CALLAHAIV

CALLAHAN

"Stop inhaling your food!"

"BAT NIGHT" AT SHEA STADIUM

CALLAHAN

"Get away from those other kids!
They're not like you!!"

CALLAHAN

CALLAHAN

CRUAHAN

THE FUNERAL OF G.W. CONWAY, FOUNDER OF THE ANIMAL RIGHTS MOVEMENT.

CALLAHAN

CALLAHAN

FREAKS OF NATURE

THE
"HONEST LAWYER"

THE
"OBEDIENT CAT"

THE
"HAPPY-GO-LUCKY
FEMINIST"

CALLAHAN

MAPS TO THE HOMES OF THE STARS WHO STILL CLING TO HOLLYWOOD LEFTIST POLITICS!

CALLAHAN

CALLAHAN

CALLAHAN

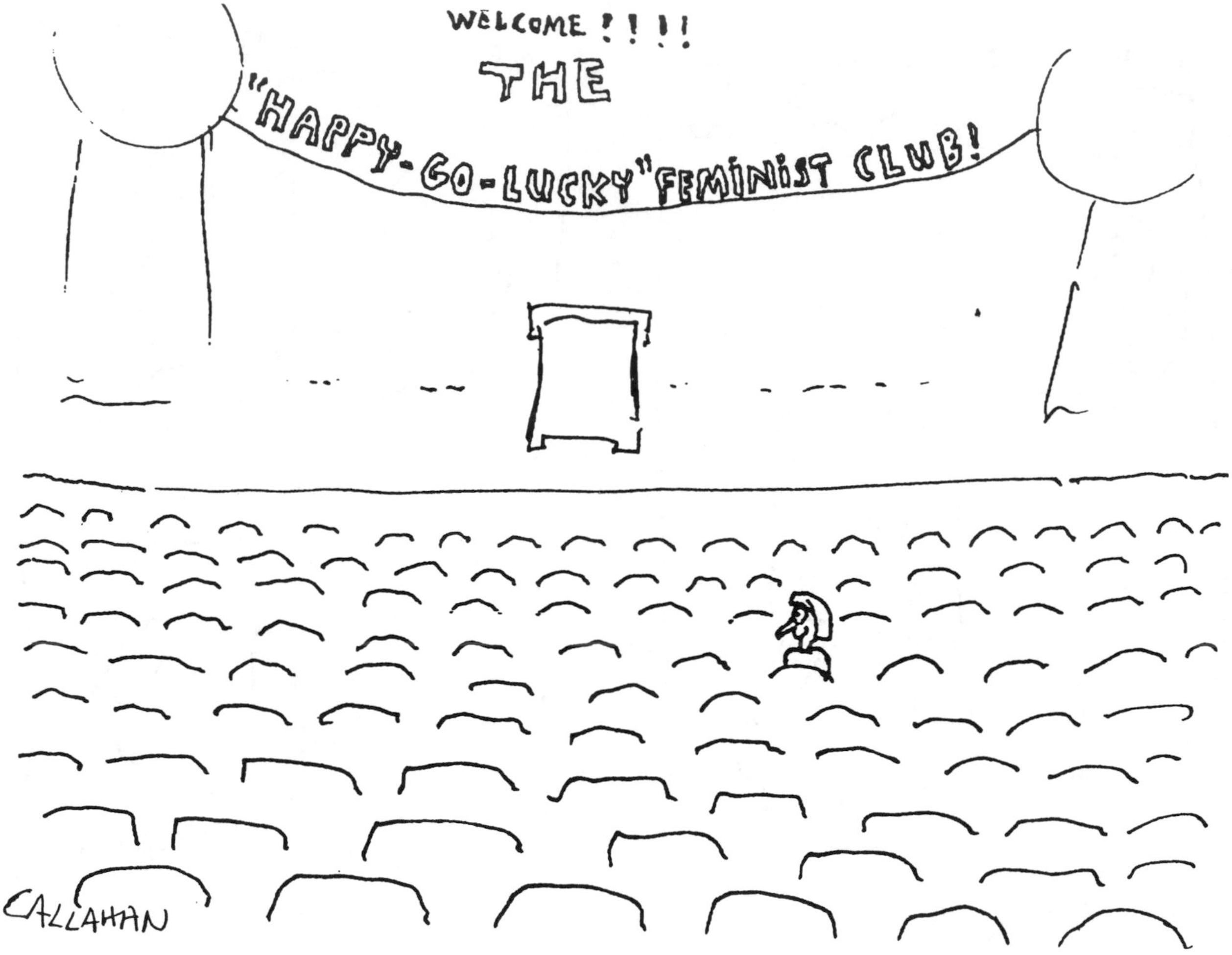
WELCOME !!!!
THE
"HAPPY-GO-LUCKY" FEMINIST CLUB!
CALLAHAN

CALLAHAN

"Welcome to the news. I'm Chuck Wilson substituting for Brad Stevens, who shit his pants and had to go home."

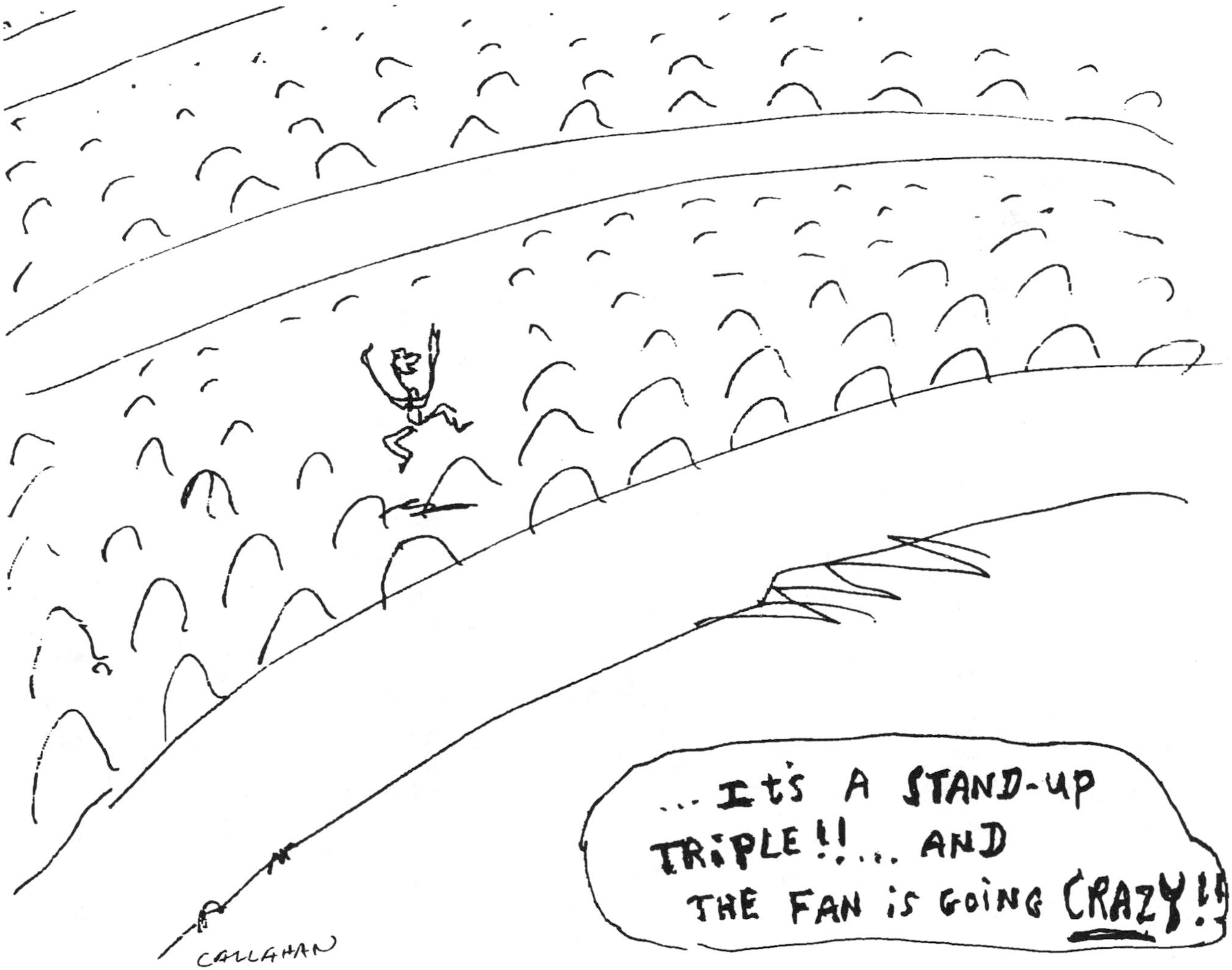
...It's A STAND-UP TRIPLE!!... AND THE FAN IS GOING CRAZY!!
CALLAHAN

ALAN DERSHOWITZ'S BRAIN

Larry King show

Being on the Larry King show 98%

ethics 2%

CALLAHAN

BAILEY

COCHRAN

SHAPIRO

CALLAHAN